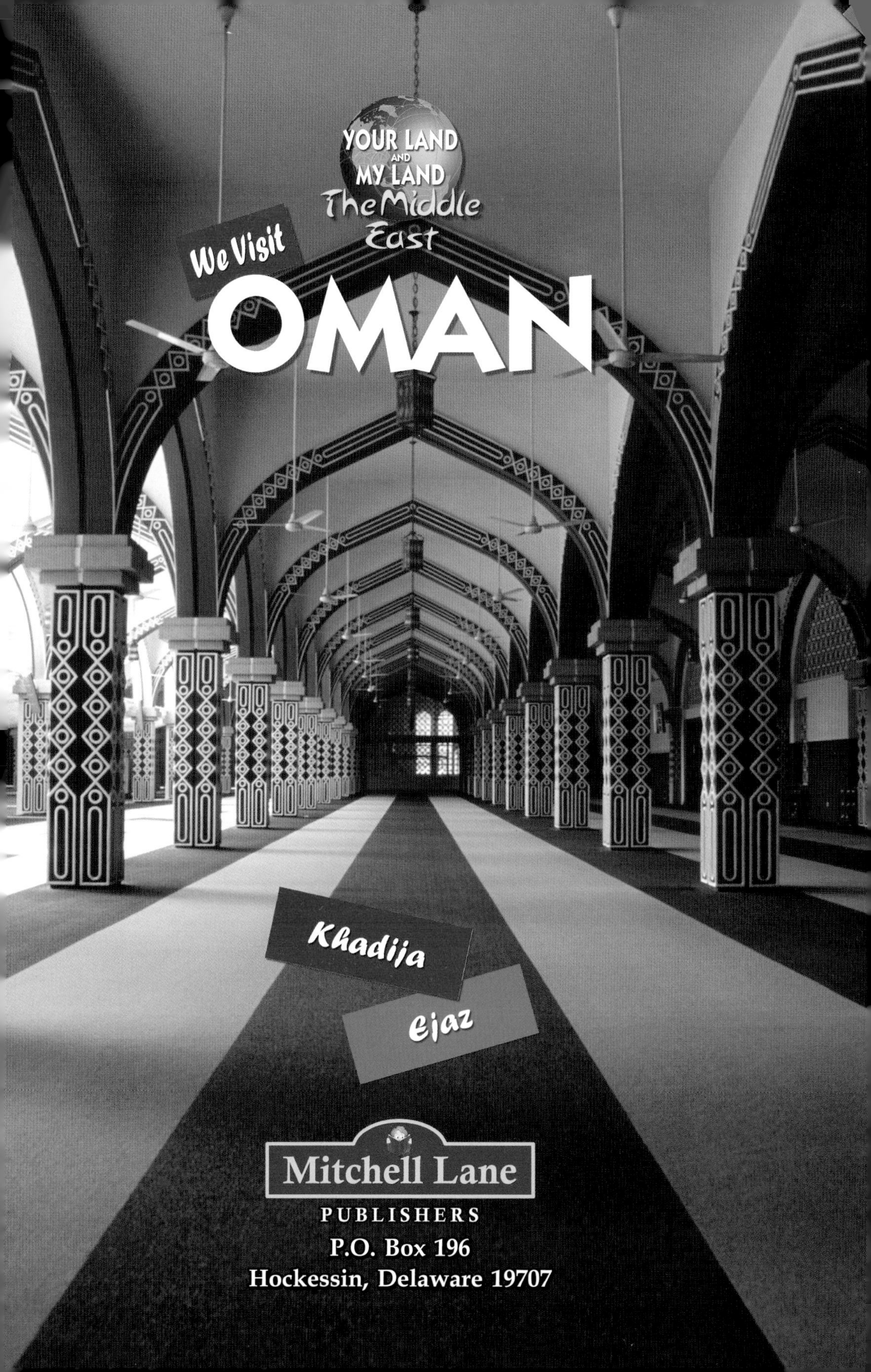

YOUR LAND
AND
MY LAND
The Middle
East

We Visit

OMAN

Khadija

Ejaz

Mitchell Lane
PUBLISHERS

P.O. Box 196
Hockessin, Delaware 19707

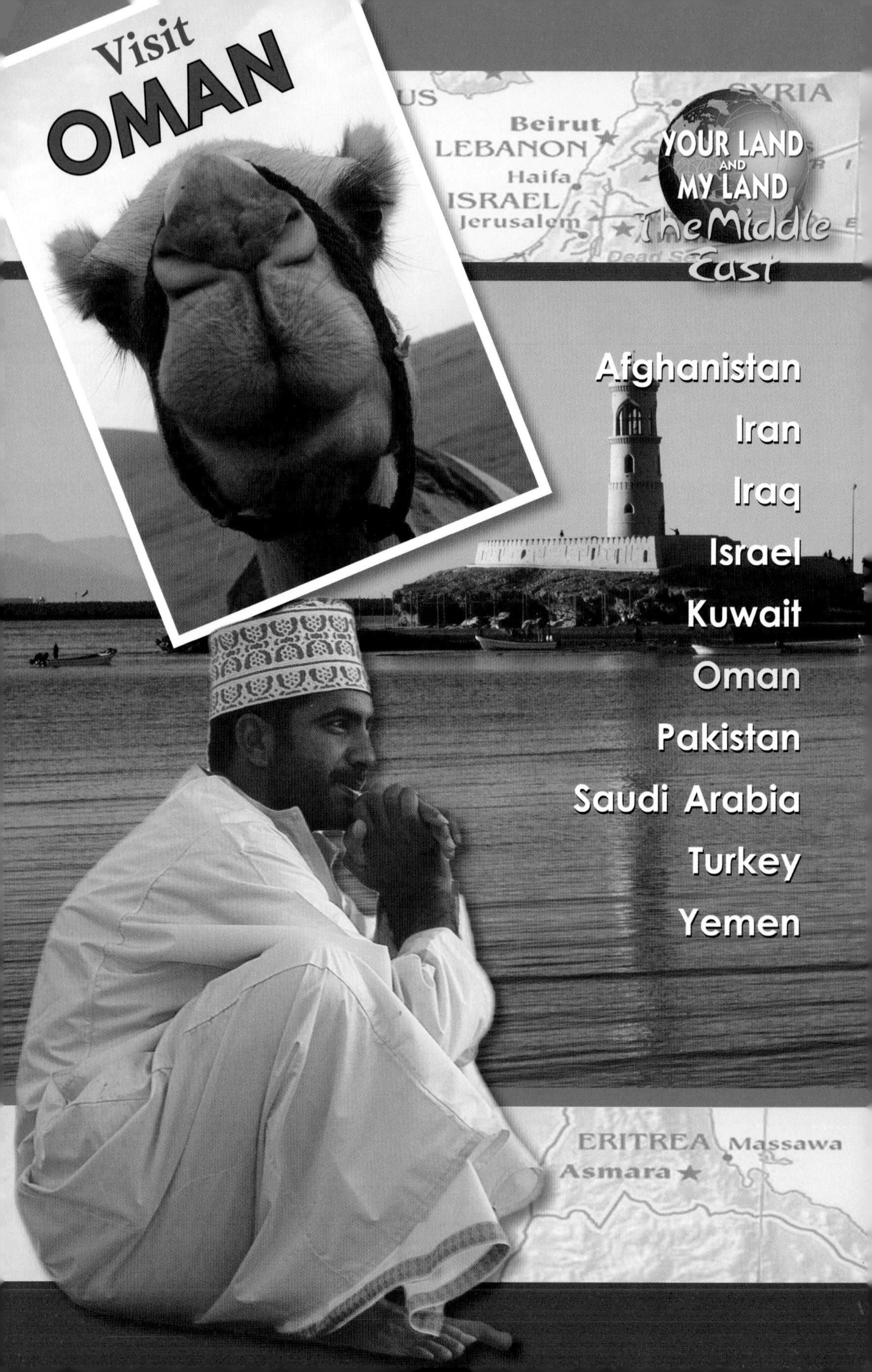
Visit
OMAN
Beirut
LEBANON
Haifa
ISRAEL
Jerusalem
SYRIA
YOUR LAND AND MY LAND
The Middle East
Afghanistan
Iran
Iraq
Israel
Kuwait
Oman
Pakistan
Saudi Arabia
Turkey
Yemen
ERITREA
Massawa
Asmara

YOUR LAND
AND
MY LAND
The Middle
East

We Visit

OMAN

Printing   1   2   3   4   5   6   7   8   9

Library of Congress Cataloging-in-Publication Data
Ejaz, Khadija.
 We visit Oman / by Khadija Ejaz.
     p. cm. — (Your land and my land—the Middle East)
 Includes bibliographical references and index.
 ISBN 978-1-58415-962-9 (library bound)
 1. Oman—Juvenile literature. I. Title.
 DS247.O6E37 2011
 953.53—dc22
                                                                    2011000724

eBook ISBN: 9781612281049

PUBLISHER'S NOTE: This story is based on the author's extensive research, which she believes to be accurate. Documentation of this research is on page 61.

The Internet sites referenced herein were active as of the publication date. Due to the fleeting nature of some web sites, we cannot guarantee they will all be active when you are reading this book.

To reflect current usage, we have chosen to use the secular era designations BCE ("before the common era") and CE ("of the common era") instead of the traditional designations BC ("before Christ") and AD (*anno Domini,* "in the year of the Lord").

PLB

Contents

Introduction

Do you know the difference between the Middle East, the Arab World, the Muslim World, and the Gulf States? Some countries fall under more than one of these categories.

Traditionally, the Middle East has referred to the region that separates Europe and Africa from Asia. The modern-day countries that make up this region are Turkey, Bahrain, Kuwait, Oman, Qatar, Saudi Arabia, the United Arab Emirates (UAE), Yemen, Iraq, Israel, Jordan, Lebanon, Syria, Iran, Cyprus, and Egypt. Britain and France carved many of these countries from the territories of the Ottoman Empire after it collapsed during World War I.[1]

The Middle East forms the heart of the Arab World—that is, the countries where most of the people speak Arabic, regardless of their religion. Many countries in North Africa, such as Sudan, Algeria, Morocco, and Tunisia, fall under this category. Many Jews and Christians from these countries are native Arabic speakers, too.

The Muslim World includes countries where Islam is a major religion. This includes African, Asian, and European countries, such as

غرفة الصلاة للنساة
LADIES PRAYER ROOM

Nigeria, Pakistan, Afghanistan, Indonesia, and Albania. Even India and Russia have significant Muslim populations.[2]

The Gulf States are the six Arab monarchial countries around the Persian Gulf. These countries are Saudi Arabia, the UAE, Qatar, Bahrain, Kuwait, and Oman.

Is the country in this book part of the Arab World? The Muslim world? Both? Is it also one of the Gulf States? What is its connection to the Middle East? Turn the page and let's find out!

The Sultan Qaboos Grand Mosque in Muscat is just one of the many beautiful buildings in the country's capital. The mosque took over six years to build. It was dedicated in 2001.

Oman
Overview

Welcome to the Sultanate of Oman! You might be surprised to know that, as recently as 1970, many people in the world had not even heard of this country. Despite a rich past that included numerous civilizations and a seafaring empire, Oman had fallen into isolation after a period of political decline in the early and mid twentieth century. By 1970, Oman had no diplomats abroad—the country was closed to the outside world.

A lot was happening outside of Oman at that time. The world was entering the Space Age. In 1970, the Concorde made its first supersonic flight, and Pan American Airlines put the first Boeing 747 into service. The Beatles split up that year, and the North Tower of the World Trade Center became the tallest building in the world. Oil had already been discovered in the Middle East, and the winds of change had begun sweeping across that ancient part of the world that had lain in disrepair since the world wars. The face of the Middle East was changing, and very swiftly so.

From far away on the southeastern edge of the Arabian Peninsula, the ruler of Oman found these changes unsettling. Sultan Said bin Taimur bin Feisal al Said wanted to protect his people's way of life, so he monitored all the comings and goings of his kingdom very carefully. Nothing could happen in his country without his knowing.

The Oman of those days was very different from its modern incarnation. Its untamed and sparsely populated terrain was reminiscent of the American Wild West. Oman had no TVs, and radios were banned by the government. In 1970, Oman only had 6 miles (10 kilometers) of paved roads, one hospital with 12 beds, and 3 schools.[1] A handful of boys and no girls were in school; Omani society was mostly uneducated and fiercely tribal. People traveled by donkey, camel, and on foot. There was no international airport, just one narrow airstrip.[2]

The country even had a different name—Muscat and Oman. Muscat was the capital city and was housed within high walls. With the boom of cannon fire, its gates would close at sunset and remain so until sunrise. Those who wandered outside in the dark risked being shot by guards. The ones who managed to get permission to go outside had to carry lanterns so that they could show the guards their faces.[3] Flashlights were not allowed because they could be used to blind the guards.[1]

Despite his precautions, the winds of change that Sultan Said so feared eventually found their way into his kingdom. On July 23, 1970, Sultan Said was deposed in a bloodless palace coup by his son, Qaboos bin Said bin Taimur al Said. Sultan Said was sent into exile in the United Kingdom, where he died two years later. It was his son who brought Oman out of isolation and opened it to modernization and to the world.

Today, most people have a hard time imagining such a tumultuous period in Oman's recent history. Muscat is the pride of the country, a swiftly expanding modern city that has long since spilled over its old walls, which still stand as a reminder of the nation's rebirth. The Omani people never pursued development at the cost of their heritage though, and today, their country comfortably exists in harmony with its past and its present with an eager eye on the future.

Oman shares its modern borders with Yemen in the southwest, Saudi Arabia in the west, and the United Arab Emirates (UAE) in the northwest. The Sultanate's border runs along the Strait of Hormuz in the north, the Gulf of Oman in the northeast, and the Arabian Sea in the east and the south.[4] Muscat, Sohar, Sur, and Nizwa in the north and Salalah in the south are some of its major cities.

Oman also contains two exclaves, Musandam and Madhi, separated from the rest of the country by the UAE. In addition, Oman has sovereignty over a number of small islands (inhabited or otherwise)

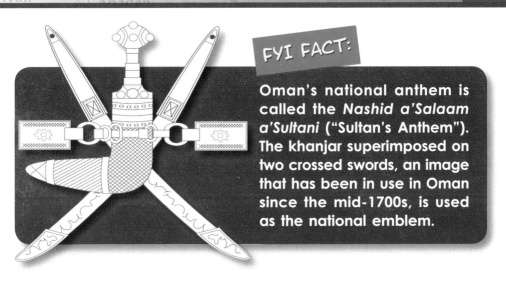

Oman's national anthem is called the *Nashid a'Salaam a'Sultani* ("Sultan's Anthem"). The khanjar superimposed on two crossed swords, an image that has been in use in Oman since the mid-1700s, is used as the national emblem.

along its coastline, including Salamah and Her Daughters; Masirah; and the Hallaniyat islands.[5]

The country is divided into four governorates (Muscat, Dhofar, Musandam, and Buraymi) and five regions (Batinah, Dhahirah/Zahirah, Dakhiliyah, Sharqiyah, and Wusta). Dhofar is the largest, and the Batinah is the most fertile. Half the population of Oman lives in the Batinah and Muscat areas alone, making that part of the country the most densely populated. The governorates and regions are further divided into a total of 61 *wilayats,* each of which is overseen by a *wali,* a government official who is responsible for collecting taxes and maintaining the peace.

Oman's transformation into a modern nation is credited to the leadership and vision of its monarch, His Majesty (HM) Sultan Qaboos. Soon after he ascended the throne in 1970, he used the money from the sale of Omani oil to build schools, hospitals, and roads, and to improve the living conditions of his people. Girls especially were encouraged to attend school, and both boys and girls were given access to learn English and, later, computers. As of 2009, Oman had 14,508 miles (23,349 kilometers) of paved roads; 1,283 schools (including international schools and those for children with special needs); 58 hospitals; and 933 health centers, units, and clinics. It had two airports with four more in the works and even its own international airlines.[5] And the country is still growing.

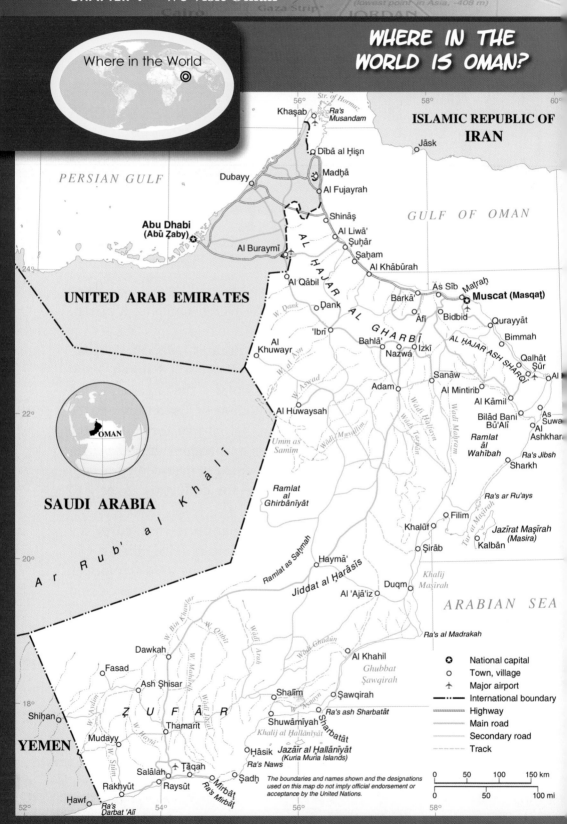

WHERE IN THE WORLD IS OMAN?

Where in the World

ISLAMIC REPUBLIC OF **IRAN**

PERSIAN GULF

GULF OF OMAN

Str. of Hormuz

Khaṣab
Ra's Musandam
Jāsk
Dībā al Ḥiṣn
Madḥā
Dubayy
Al Fujayrah
Abu Dhabi (Abū Ẓaby)
Shināṣ
Al Liwā'
Ṣuḥār
Al Buraymī
Saham
Al Khābūrah
Āṣ Sīb   Maṭraḥ
Muscat (Masqaṭ)
Al Qābil
Barkā
Dank
Āfī   Bidbid
Qurayyāt

UNITED ARAB EMIRATES

W. Dank

AL HAJAR AL GHARBĪ

Bimmah

'Ibrī
Bahlā   Izkī   Nazwā
AL HAJAR ASH SHARQĪ
Qalhāt   Ṣūr
Al Khuwayr
W. al Ayn
Sanāw
Adam   Al Mintirib
Al Kāmil
Al Huwaysah
W. Aswad
Wādī Ḥalfayn
Wādī Tayin
Wādī Mahram
Bilād Bani Bū 'Alī
As Suwa
Al Ashkhar
Ramlat āl Waḥībah
Ra's Jibsh
Sharkh

OMAN

Umm as Samīm   Wādī Musallim

Ramlat al Ghirbānīyāt

SAUDI ARABIA

Ra's ar Ru'ays

Khalūf   Filim
Jazīrat Maṣīrah (Masira)
Ṣirāb   Kalbān
Khalīj Maṣīrah

Tur al Maṣīrah

Ramlat as Sạhmah
Haymā'
Jiddat al Ḥarāsīs
Al 'Ajā'iz   Duqm

ARABIAN SEA

Ra's al Madrakah

W. Bin Khawlar   W. Qitbit
Dawkah
W. Maharib
Wādī 'Arah
Wādī Ghadūn
Al Khahil
Ghubbat Ṣawqirah
Fasad
Ash Shisar
Shalim   Ṣawqirah
Ra's ash Sharbatāt
Shuwāmīyah   Sharbatāt
Shihan
Z U F Ā R
Thamarīt
W. Aydim   W. Nahiz
Khalīj al Ḥallānīyāt
Mudayy
W. Sinn
Ḥāsik   Jazā'ir al Ḥallānīyāt (Kuria Muria Islands)
Ra's Naws

YEMEN

Salālah   Ṭāqah
Rakhyūt   Raysūt   Ṣadḥ
Hawf   Ra's Mirbāt
Ra's Ḍarbat 'Alī

Ar Rub' al Khālī

Al Buraymī

Ra's Mirbāt
Mirbāt

O   National capital
o   Town, village
✈   Major airport
━ ∙ ━   International boundary
▨▨▨   Highway
───   Main road
───   Secondary road
- - -   Track

0   50   100   150 km
0   50   100 mi

The boundaries and names shown and the designations used on this map do not imply official endorsement or acceptance by the United Nations.

OMAN FACTS AT A GLANCE

Flag of Oman

Full name: Sultanate of Oman

Official language: Arabic

Population: 2,967,717 (includes 577,293 non-nationals) (July 2010 estimate)

Land area: 119,499 square miles (309,500 square kilometers); roughly the size of Kansas

Capital: Muscat

Government: Monarchy

Ethnic makeup: Arab, Baluchi, South Asian (Indian, Pakistani, Sri Lankan, Bangladeshi), African

Religions: Ibadhi Muslim 75%, other (includes Sunni Muslim, Shia Muslim, Hindu, Christian, etc.) 25%

Exports: Petroleum, re-exports, fish, metals, textiles

Imports: Machinery and transportation equipment, manufactured goods, food, livestock, lubricants

Crops: Dates, limes, bananas, alfalfa, vegetables

Average temperatures: August 90°F (32°C); January 70°F (21°C)

Average rainfall: 4 inches (10 cm)

Highest point: Jabal Shams—9,777 feet (2,980 meters)

Flag: The flag was introduced in 1970. It bears three horizontal bands of white, red, and green of equal width with a broad, vertical red band on the hoist side. The national emblem (a khanjar in its sheath superimposed on two crossed swords in scabbards) in white is centered near the top of the vertical band.

Source: CIA *World Factbook:* "Oman"

Frankincense is extracted from the trunk of the *Boswellia sacra* tree in the form of a sticky, milky fluid (pictured, upper left), which hardens after extraction. Oman produces four types of frankincense: hawjari, najdi, shazri, and sahli.

Chapter

2

Since the Time of Frankincense

Once upon a time, the south of Oman was the center of the world. The lonely frankincense tree that still marks the landscape of the southern region of Dhofar bears witness to a time when frankincense was a prized commodity all around the ancient world, guarded as jealously as gold is today. The Assyrians wanted it, the Romans wanted it, and even the three wise men chose to give it to Mary (Maryam in Arabic) upon the birth of her son, Jesus (Isa).[1]

Unique and expensive, Dhofari frankincense has been a brand of its own since ancient times, claiming Balqis, the Queen of Sheba (Saba, a region in modern-day Yemen), as one of its most famous regular customers. The Romans used to burn Dhofari incense when they swore oaths of loyalty to their emperor, and people from all over the ancient world used it in their funerary rituals. Today, frankincense is a key ingredient of Amouage, an Omani perfume that is one of the most expensive in the world.[2]

Many historians and theologians believe that the prosperous city of Ophir that is mentioned in the Bible may have been Dhofar. It is said that the cities of Ophir were made of gold and that King Solomon received expensive and exotic shipments from there.[1]

Quinquireme of Nineveh from distant Ophir, / Rowing home to haven in sunny Palestine, / With a cargo of ivory, / And apes and peacocks, / Sandalwood, cedarwood, and sweet white wine. —John Masefield, 1878–1967

UNESCO has listed a number of Omani archaeological sites as World Heritage Sites. These include the necropolis at Bat, Al Khutm, and Al Ayn, and the ancient frankincense routes at Shisr (Wubar), Khor Rori (Sumhurum), Al Baleed, and Wadi Dawkah.[3] At Sumhurum are said to be the remains of the palace of Queen Balqis, where she used to stay while in town to buy frankincense. The legendary region of Wubar had been built by the people of 'Ad. Its city, Iram, is mentioned in the Quran.

> Do you not see how your Lord
> dealt with the 'Ad [people],
> Of the [city of] Iram, with lofty pillars,
> The likes of which were not produced
> in [all] the land?
> —Quran 89:6-8, *surah Al Fajr* (The Dawn)

Standing in the midst of the ruins of Wubar with one's eyes closed can be a magical experience. If one tries hard enough, the silence will be transformed into the bustle of a great trading post from the past. Once more will the caravans stream in to this corner of the Arabian Peninsula, laden with delectable spices, exotic creatures, and intricate handicrafts from all parts of the ancient world—Rome, Assyria, and Egypt.

The ruins of the Wubarite oasis and its collapsed well-spring. Iram was the town of the people of 'Ad that was eventually discovered in the 1990s.

Oman is located on the southeastern coast of the Arabian Peninsula, a region the Romans used to call *Arabia Felix,* or Fortunate Arabia. The Arabian Peninsula has also been called Arabistan, the Arabian subcontinent, or simply Arabia. The peninsula itself lies on a tectonic plate called the Arabian Plate.[4]

The rocks in Oman have been dated to at least 825 million years ago—the oldest ones are found in Duqm and Nafun in the Wusta region.[5] Oman was covered by ice in at least three periods in the past, and evidence also suggests that this part of the peninsula was once attached to Africa.[4] Parts of Oman were once under water, a fact that is supported by the presence of fossilized shells and sedimentary rock formations in the interior regions of the country.[2]

Geography had a hand in shaping Oman's history. A unique combination of geographical features ensured that the natives maintained a distinct identity. The country's strategic position on ancient trade routes and its proximity to the sea also predestined the natives for travel over the land and seas. Oman's political history has also oscillated between claims to power from local tribes and from foreign forces.[6]

Hunting, fishing, and agricultural communities inhabited Oman as long ago as 10,000 BCE. Some of the ancient cultures that occupied Oman were Hafit, Lizq, Umm a'Nar, Wadi Suq, Samad, and Wubar. Many of these cultures had organized economic and political links with the outside world.

Some of Oman's ancient trading partners were China, India, Mesopotamia, the Mediterranean, the Nile Valley, and East Africa.[3] Ancient Sumerian cuneiform texts refer to Oman as Magan or Makkan. The name indicates shipbuilding and copper smelting, a reference to the copper and diorite the Omani ships would supply to Mesopotamia four thousand years ago.[3]

From the sixth century BCE until the seventh century CE, Oman was part of the Persian Empire. The Persians called Oman Mazoon, a name derived from *muzn* (clouds and heavy rain), referring to Oman's abundant supply of water in the past. Some historians suggest Oman got its name from Uman, a place in modern Yemen from which some of the Omani tribes came.[1] Others say that the name comes from the son of the prophet Abraham (Ibrahim), or the son of Abraham's son, Joktan.[4]

Oman was one of the first countries to accept Islam when Jaifar and Abd, the joint rulers of Oman at the time, were invited to Islam in 630 CE by Amr bin al As, a messenger from the Prophet Muhammad.[4] The first Omani Muslim was Mazin bin Ghadouba, who had traveled to Mecca and met the Prophet.[1] Oman also played an important role in bringing the message of Islam to other nations, particularly along its trading routes to Asia and Africa.

Far atop the Western Hajar Mountains on a 650-foot- (200-meter-) high peak rests the Nakhl Fort. Its construction dates back to the pre-Islamic period, and it has been restored a number of times.

An Empire by the Sea

The forts of Oman have many tales to tell. Just taking in the view from atop one can be an exhilarating experience. The battlements one may graze with a light touch may have been the exact spot where a soldier once bravely held his position during a losing battle. Maybe it was a young king who stood there instead, pausing during a nighttime stroll as he took in the same landscape, his kingdom, his responsibilities, his fatigue. A walk along the corridors of these majestic stone structures may even feel like time travel as visitors relive the memory of ancient intrigues. There are over 500 forts all across Oman, and each one awaits a visitor to live its story all over again.

The fort in Nizwa is the largest in Arabia, and it stands distinct with its massive round tower. The Bahla fort is listed with UNESCO as a World Heritage Site.[1] Some forts have been converted into museums: the Bait al Falaj fort now houses the Armed Forces Museum. Used as a prison until the early 1970s, Fort Jalali too is now a museum. It watches over the Al Alam Royal Palace in Muscat with its twin, Fort Merani, at the entrance of the crescent-shaped Muscat Bay. Just outside Muscat, the Muttrah fort overlooks the seaside drive of Corniche from the mountains. Other major forts are located in Sohar, Nakhl, Jabrin, and Rustaq.

Nizwa was also the center of the Muslim Ibadhi imamate, which the Omanis established in 751; the first publicly elected Omani imam was Julanda bin Masud. The founder of Ibadhism, Jabir bin Zaid al Azdi, was also from Nizwa. From this time on, the imam, an elected spiritual leader from the interior regions, would frequently struggle with the king from the coast for political control. Difficulty in electing an imam would also cause conflicts between tribes.

From 661 to 1154, Oman prospered but was intermittently ruled by the Umayyads, Abbasids, Qarmatians, Buyids, and Seljuqs of Kirman. By 1154, the indigenous Nabhan dynasty had established control over Oman. They stayed in power until 1624, but their rule was marked by political unrest from both internal and external sources. The Persians were particularly active in their aggressions against them.[2] These conflicts weakened Oman and attracted the attention of European explorers and colonizers.

Famous travelers such as Ibn Battuta and Marco Polo passed through Oman. Ibn Battuta was a famous fourteenth-century Moroccan Muslim who is known to have traveled more than Marco Polo. His book *Rihla* (Voyage) is his personal record of nearly thirty years of travel over Africa, Europe, the Middle East, and Asia. Marco Polo was particularly impressed with Qalhat, a city later destroyed by the Portuguese under Alfonso de Albuquerque. History buffs can still visit its ruins, especially the remains of the Bibi Maryam mausoleum, which was built of fossilized coral and decorated with plasterwork.[3]

Portugal invaded Muscat in 1507 and Hormuz in 1515. It occupied the coast and took control of the trade routes there. By 1650, the Omanis were able to unite under Imam Nasir bin Murshid bin Sultan al Yarubi and drive the Portuguese away, ushering in the prosperous Yarubi period (1624–1744).[4] The Yarubis united Oman into the first and now oldest independent state in Arabia, and Oman was able to extend its fleet and dominate trade on the Indian Ocean.[5]

By the latter part of the Yarubi period, Oman was once again plagued with political conflicts, especially with the Ottomans and the Persians. Ahmed bin Said bin Ahmed al Busaidi, the governor of Sohar, united the Omanis and expelled the Ottomans and the Persians. He was elected imam in 1744 and founded the Busaidi (Al Bu Said) dynasty, which has lasted into the twenty-first century. The monarchial coast and the imamate interior were united under the name of Muscat and Oman, and no foreign power has occupied the country since.

Oman's maritime activities were revived under the Busaidis, who adopted the title of Sultan and moved the capital from Rustaq to Muscat in 1793.[6] The Busaidis were also the first to use the titles of Sayyid (Lord) and Sayyida (Lady).[7] The Omani Empire reached the height of its power in the mid-nineteenth century to include Zanzibar and Mombasa in Africa and also parts of Persia, Pakistan, and India. Political links were established with the French, British, and Dutch. The French and the British particularly rivaled each other for control over Oman. In 1832, Zanzibar became the second capital of the empire and witnessed a period of rebirth.

An Omani shield. Many a brave Omani has defended his tribe and his nation with armor and weaponry like this shield.

In 1856, the Omani Empire was divided between two quarreling princes—Majid and Thuwaini, the sons of the great Busaidi ruler Said bin Sultan bin Ahmad al Said (Said the Great). Majid took Zanzibar, and Thuwaini took Muscat and Oman. Over time, Muscat and Oman declined into political instability and poverty as the imam resumed clashes with the sultan. The last imam, Ghalib bin Ali al Hinai, was expelled by the sultan in 1959 with the help of Great Britain.[7]

In 1965, communist rebels formed the Dhofar Liberation Front. HM Sultan Qaboos ascended to the throne in 1970 and put the rebellion to rest in 1975 with help from Jordan and Iran. The new ruler changed the name of the country from Muscat and Oman to the Sultanate of Oman and opened the country to development.

The Jabal Akhdar Mountains are located in the north of Oman. The ancient Arab tribe of the Bani Riyam lives here, but many of its descendants now live nearby in towns like Nizwa, Izki, and Ibra.

Extreme Geography

Hiking enthusiasts who make it to the peak of Jabal Shams often feel as if they can reach out and touch the sky. At 9,777 feet (2,980 meters) above sea level, the "Mountain of the Sun" is the highest point in Oman and in Eastern Arabia. It is also a part of the Jabal Akhdar (Green Mountain) sub range of the rocky Hajar Mountains in northern Oman.[1] Like a cool oasis in the middle of a harsh desert, the Jabal Akhdar thrills visitors with its lush green slopes, showing a diverse terrain that shatters the stereotype of the barren Arabian desert.

The Sumail Gap divides the Hajar Mountains into a western range (Hajar al Gharbi) and an eastern range (Hajar al Sharqi). Numerous fjords cross the Hajar in Musandam, which has earned that region the nickname of the Norway of the Middle East.[2] Natives have long compared the craggy Hajar to a human backbone, and many have even called it the Grand Canyon of Oman. A beautiful sense of poetry can be seen in how the Omanis named their land. North of the Hajar Mountains, the Batinah (meaning "inner" or "front") is called the belly of the country, and in the south, the Dhahirah means "the back."[3]

South of the Hajar Mountains lie the deserts of the Rub al-Khali (Empty Quarter) and the Wahiba Sands, also called the Sharqiyah (Eastern) Sands. The Rub al Khali is a gravel desert located in the central and western parts of Oman. The Wahiba Sands, in contrast, is a sandy desert in eastern Oman. Many have called it a sea of sand, comparing its shifting dunes to the ever-changing waves of an ocean.

The Qara Mountains, a continuous range smaller than the Hajar, occupy the south.

Nature lovers can lose themselves in a variety of activities across the diverse geography of Oman. Wadi-bashing and dune-bashing, where people drive four-wheelers into dry wadis and across sand dunes, have grown into popular leisure sports, as has sand-skiing. The Al Hota caves and the Majlis al Jinn (Meeting Room of the Spirits) are popular rock climbing and cave exploration spots. The Majlis al Jinn is the second-largest underground chamber in the world.[4]

Oman's geography can also be split between the interior and the coast. Some of the world's cleanest and most beautiful beaches, bays, lagoons (*khawr*), creeks, headlands, and islands can be found along Oman's coastline.[1] Scientists have discovered numerous unique ecosystems and an incredibly diverse marine life along the mangroves, kelp beds, and coral reefs on this coast.[4]

Visitors can locate the Majlis al Jinn in a remote area of the Selma Plateau. Its largest entrances are called Asterisk (Khoshilat Beya al Hiyool) and First Drop (Khoshilat Maqandeli). The smallest entry is called Cheryl's Drop (Khoshilat Minqod).

Oman's beautiful beaches attract those with a passion for water sports, including surfing, scuba diving, snorkeling, and sailing. Visitors can also opt for dolphin and whale watching tours.[2] During high tide at Mughsayl in Dhofar, seawater rushes through blowholes in the limestone rocks to form fountains.[4] In Sur, the turtle sanctuaries in Ras al Hadd offer tourists the rare sight of turtles coming onto the beach to lay their eggs.[2] The hot springs at Rustaq and Nakhl and the cold springs at Ain Razat and Salalah also draw many visitors.[5] Rustaq's hot springs are rumored to have healing properties.[3]

While in Rustaq, visitors might also want to check out the remains of the house and clinic of a famous Omani doctor. Rashid bin Umaira bin Thani gained fame for his work in classic Omani medicine in the fifteenth century.[3] Another famous Omani doctor was Abu Muhammad Abdellah bin Muhammad al Azdi from Sohar. Also called Ibn al Thahabi,[6] he compiled the first known alphabetical medical encyclopedia, *Kitab al Ma'a* (The Book of Water), in the eleventh century. Both of these doctors documented many diseases, including heart disease, cancer, and psychological disorders. They also listed treatments and described the functioning of various organs.[3]

The Tropic of Cancer passes through Oman, and while most of the country is arid, the southern region of Dhofar is more tropical. The diverse terrain also makes the interior regions extremely hot and dry and the coastal areas very humid.

The Omani sky is generally blue and sunny all year round. The summer months from May to September tend to get very hot, especially in the north, with temperatures reaching 130°F (55°C) in the shade. Winters from October to April are mild and pleasant.[2] In the sandy desert of the Wahiba, scientists have recorded a temperature range of 130°F (55°C) during the day to near freezing at night.[4]

In Muscat, rainfall averages about 4 inches (100 millimeters) per year, but that amount is higher in the mountains. The Jabal Akhdar receives up to 35 inches (900 millimeters) of rain a year. The rainy season in the north is between November and April, but a southwestern monsoon keeps the south lush and shrouded in mist between July and August. In the desert regions, rainfall is rare and sporadic.

Aflaaj have ensured a regular water supply to Oman for centuries. Oman has two types of *aflaaj*: *Ghaily aflaaj*, which are dug close to the ground and have open channels, and *Iddi* (or *Daudi*) *aflaaj*, which are underground with covered channels.

Chapter 5

The Land and Its Resources

The artificial water channels that snake across the landscape of Oman make for some of the best picnic spots in the country. These particularly attract the visitors who want to take in the great Omani outdoors at a leisurely pace. Picnics by the *aflaaj* (singular: *falaj*) of Oman can be an idyllic affair—sunbeams trickle through the branches of the date palms and dance on your skin, the leaves of the date palms rustle in the light breeze as the water quietly flows along in the open *falaj* next to you. If the sun makes you feel warm, all you have to do is dip your hands into the *falaj* and splash your face with the cool water. It's just that simple.

Like most things in Oman, the *aflaaj* are associated with an ancient myth. The story tells how the Prophet Solomon (Sulaimaan) visited Oman on a flying carpet and ordered his servants, the *jinns,* to build 10,000 *aflaaj* in 10 days.[1] In reality, the Persians are thought to have introduced these channels, which they called qanats, to Oman around 1000 BCE. Numerous qanats on the Iranian Plateau are still in use.

Water has always been a precious resource in Oman, but despite this scarcity, the people have always been able to access it regularly, especially through the use of the *aflaaj.* In the *aflaaj,* gravity transports water from upland reservoirs to lower-lying levels.[2] Water closest to the source is used for drinking. It is extracted next for washing, and then finally for agriculture.[1] Of Oman's 4,112 *aflaaj,* 3,017 are still active. UNESCO lists five *aflaaj* as World Heritage Sites.[3]

Rainfall provides 65 percent of Oman's water supply, and the rest is derived from desalination plants.[3] Rain fills the wadis (dry riverbeds), transforming the area by creating small waterfalls. Groundwater reservoirs benefit greatly from these wadi flows.

The *aflaaj* network is also supplemented by recharge dams and wells. These dams retain the water that rushes down the wadis so that it isn't lost to the sea. This also allows more water to seep into the earth and replenish the water table.[2] Oman's 225 naturally occurring springs (both hot and cold) are also important sources of water.[4] The freshwater springs of Dhofar, for instance, flow throughout the year.[5] The availability of water is important to the people and the economy of Oman. Agriculture, livestock, and fisheries provide food, revenue, and jobs for many Omanis.[6] Oman produces some of the best dates in the region—over 200 varieties[1]—and has been exporting them worldwide for over 2,000 years. The revenue they bring in is second only to what is earned from oil.

Since their discovery in Oman in 1964, oil and natural gas have contributed the most to Oman's economy—Oman produces around 805,000 barrels of oil per day.[7] Although the Arabian Peninsula possesses oil and gas in abundance, Oman's supply is the least in the region.[8] Wanting to reduce the country's reliance on the oil sector, the government has tried to diversify the economy by promoting privatization and industrialization. Oman also earns revenue from non-oil industries such as machinery, pharmaceuticals, and the development of natural resources, and from service industries such as tourism.[9]

The Safah oil field in northern Oman. Oil is formed under the earth when layers of fossils, both animal and plant, are subjected to great pressure and temperature for millions of years. The oil from Oman's Wusta region, at 600 million years old, is some of the oldest in the world.

While the Free Trade Agreement between Oman and the United States was implemented as recently as 2009, Oman's trading history goes back much further. Seafaring Omanis were exporting copper and diorite to Mesopotamia 4,000 years ago, and around 1000 BCE, Dhofari frankincense had become an essential item in religious ceremonies in ancient Assyria, Egypt, Greece, and Rome.[7]

Today, Oman also exports petroleum, fish, metals, textiles, chemical industry products, machinery, and electrical equipment. Its mineral resources include chromium, limestone, marble, ornamental stones, silica, lead, gypsum, and iron. Jabal Akhdar is famous for its roses, which are used to make rosewater and perfume.[2]

Omani livestock consists of goats, sheep, and cows. In some parts of Oman, camel herds are still considered a status symbol, and Arab appreciation of these "ships of the desert" has inspired at least 30 words for it in the Arabic language![2] Omanis also keep bees and breed horses, ostriches, and camels.[10]

An Omani coppersmith files a copper bowl. Copperware is common in this country, where the metal has been found in abundance since ancient times.

Thanks to its long coastline, Oman has become a major supplier of fish in the region and abroad. Fish farms across the country harvest rare delicacies such as yellow-fin tuna and abalone for international export.[2] The Omanis even like to feed dried fish to their livestock.

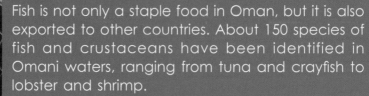

Fish is not only a staple food in Oman, but it is also exported to other countries. About 150 species of fish and crustaceans have been identified in Omani waters, ranging from tuna and crayfish to lobster and shrimp.

An oryx resting in the shade. The oryx population was wiped out in 1972 as a result of indiscriminate hunting, but they were reintroduced to Oman in 1980. They are now protected at the Arabian Oryx Sanctuary, Oman's first protected area.

The animals most commonly seen in Oman are camels and Arabian tahr mountain goats. Lynxes, sandcats, hedgehogs, porcupines, genets, mongooses, Arabian wolves, hyenas, and rodents also make up the fauna of the country. Not only is it illegal to hunt, kill, or capture any wildlife in Oman, but the country has also taken measures to protect endangered species. The Arabian oryx is protected at a sanctuary at Jiddat al Harasis in Wusta, and steps have also been taken to protect the Arabian leopard, sea turtle, Arabian and Reem gazelles, Nubian ibex, desert fox, and wild cat.[1]

Over 400 species of birds have been sighted in Oman.[1] The most common birds are golden eagles, hoopoes, and Palestine sunbirds. The country's diverse marine life includes 1,100 species of fish, 125 types of coral, 22 kinds of whales and dolphins, and 242 types of algae and other water plants.[4] In addition to desert shrubs and grass, the land also bears dates, coconuts, mangoes, bananas, frankincense, alfalfa, and citrus fruits such as limes.[1]

His Majesty Sultan Qaboos bin Said bin Taimur al Said at the Bait al Barka palace in Barka. He is the 14th-generation descendant of the founder of the Al Busaidi dynasty.

A Royal Legacy

Oman is governed by an Islamic monarchy whose head of state is called a sultan. How do you know if the sultan is home? Look at the flag on top of the palace. If it is up, he's in. Maybe you'll get lucky and visit the right palace at the right time. The sultan has a number of palaces throughout the country, and he likes to stay at different ones at various times throughout the year. The palace that attracts the most visitors though is the Al Alam Palace. Built in 1972, this beautiful palace has massive pillars plated with gold that glint in the Arabian sun, as the twin forts of Jalali and Mirani stand over it by the Muscat Bay.

HM Sultan Qaboos also meets his people directly during the Royal Tours that are conducted a number of times every year. People from all walks of life across the entire country can meet their leader face to face and tell him about their concerns.[1]

The Busaidi dynasty continues under HM Sultan Qaboos, the only son of Sultan Said, who was born in Salalah. His birthday—November 18—which coincides with the liberation of Oman from the Portuguese, is celebrated as National Day.[2] His ascension to the throne on July 23, 1970, is observed as Renaissance Day. Preparations for both holidays are undertaken weeks in advance. Oman sparkles at night from the bright multicolored lights that are draped on buildings and along highways, and the national flag and pictures of HM Sultan Qaboos are displayed everywhere. People come out with their families to enjoy the military parades, horse shows, firework displays, camel

The Qasr al Alam Royal Palace in Muscat is the official estate of the sultan of Oman. Visitors are allowed only as far as the gates. In Arabic, *Qasr* means "Palace" and *Al Alam* means "The Flag."

races, and traditional songs and dances that are held all across the country.[3]

> O Oman, since the time of the Prophet
> We are a dedicated people amongst the noblest Arabs.
> Be happy! Qaboos has come
> With the blessing of Heaven.
> —The Omani National Anthem

The sultan is a 1962 graduate of the Royal Military Academy at Sandhurst in the United Kingdom. He trained with an infantry battalion in West Germany for six months before joining the British Army staff, where he studied local government for a year. Upon his return to Salalah in 1964, he began to study Shariah law and Omani history under the guidance of his father and his personal adviser, Major F. C. L. Chauncey.[1] Major Chauncey had previously served in Muscat as British Consul.[4]

HM Sultan Qaboos's interests include Arabic, art, photography, music, culture, religion, astronomy, and the environment. He reads widely and is fond of horses. He also enjoys desert camping, flying, sailing, shooting, and tennis. Since 1989, UNESCO has been awarding the Sultan Qaboos Prize for Environmental Conservation every two years.[1]

As of early 2011, Oman had no political or opposition parties. The sultan is the highest and final authority and the Supreme Commander of the Armed Forces. A number of specialized councils, institutions, and authorities—including a cabinet of ministers—advise the sultan on important matters.[5]

The Basic Law is the first document of its kind in the history of Oman. Introduced in 1996, its 81 articles, which are organized into 7 chapters, outline the principles upon which the modern state of Oman was founded. Basic Law declares that Oman is an "independent, Arab, Islamic, fully sovereign state" and that "Islamic Shariah is the basis of legislation." Laws are made with citizen participation on the basis of "justice, *shura* (consultation) and equality."[5]

Oman has a bicameral *shura* system. The Majlis Oman (Council of Oman) consists of the Majlis a'Dawla (State Council) and the Majlis a'Shura (Consultative Council). Its members serve four-year renewable terms. The State Council was established in 1997, and its members are appointed by the sultan. In 2009, 14 of its 72 members were women.[5]

The Consultative Council was created in 1991, and its members represent the various *wilayats* of the country. Since the first general election in 2003, members have been elected by Omani citizens (both men and women) over the age of 21. Two women were elected in 2003, and after the election of 2007, the Consultative Council had 84 members.[5]

A number of courts, including the Supreme Court based in Muscat, work together with the Royal Oman Police to maintain law and order in the country.[5] National security is provided by the Sultan's Armed Forces (SAF), which include the Royal Army of Oman, Royal Air Force of Oman (RAFO), and Royal Navy of Oman. These are supported by the Royal Guard of Oman (RGO). The RGO boasts the Red Helmets motorcycle team, the Free Fall parachute team, the Royal Stables, and three military bands that frequently perform at home and abroad.[1]

Omani thoroughbred camels are used by the Royal Oman Police to patrol inaccessible areas, like difficult terrain and the desert. Oman also has the world's only camel-backed bagpipe military band.

Half of the world's seaborne oil passes through the Strait of Hormuz, placing Oman in a strategic location. The country takes care to base its foreign relations on a policy of mutual respect and non-interference.[6] HM Sultan Qaboos is well-known for his reliance on dialogue to settle disputes—in 1998, thirty-three American academic institutions collectively granted him the International Peace Prize, and in 2000, he was awarded the Italian Presidential Medal in recognition of his work toward world peace.[1]

Gulf nationalism is important to Oman. In 1981, the country became a founding member of the Arab Gulf Cooperation Council (GCC). Bahrain, Kuwait, Qatar, Saudi Arabia, and the UAE are the other members of the GCC.[6] Oman is also dedicated to promoting peace in the Middle East.[5]

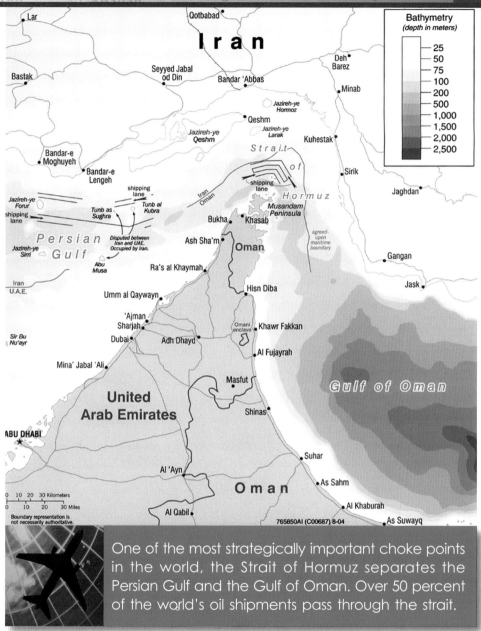

One of the most strategically important choke points in the world, the Strait of Hormuz separates the Persian Gulf and the Gulf of Oman. Over 50 percent of the world's oil shipments pass through the strait.

Oman joined the United Nations (UN) in 1971 and is also active in a number of international organizations like the Arab League, International Monetary Fund, Interpol, International Olympic Committee, Non-Aligned Movement, Organization of the Islamic Conference, World Trade Organization, and World Health Organization.

Omani coffee (*kahwah*) is made from freshly roasted ground coffee mixed with cardamom powder. Sweet *halwa* is used to balance the bitterness of the coffee.

Arab Generosity

The Omanis are a spirited and proud people, and they are famous for the generosity they extend to their guests. Visitors are warmly welcomed with a platter of Omani dates, *halwa* (sweet jelly), and black Omani coffee called *kahwah.* The sweetness of the dates and the *halwa* balances the bitterness of the *kahwah,* a hot drink that tricks the body into cooling itself in this hot country. The Omanis even have an old saying—"If you come as a friend, we are as sweet as the dates and the *halwa* we give you; but if you come as an enemy, we are as bitter as the coffee."[1]

The Arabian coffee pot is a well-known symbol of Arab hospitality. The *kahwah* is poured into *finjaan,* which are small cups that have no handles. Drinkers can shake their cups from side to side to indicate when they have had enough.

Guests are also treated to delicious combinations of rice with beef, mutton, goat, chicken, or fish. Pork is not eaten because, like alcohol, it is forbidden in Islam. Kebabs and curries (vegetable or meat) are also served with thin Omani bread called *khubz rakhal,* which can be plain or flavored with dates, sesame, thyme, and garlic.[1]

Traditional Omani foods

Most Omanis are Arab, a word that means "nomad."[2] The Arabs are a Semitic people[3] who trace their lineage to either the Qahtan tribe from southern Arabia or the Adnan tribe from the north. Other Omanis are of Baluchi, South Asian, or African descent. Foreign nationals make up one fifth of Oman's total population.

Arabic is the official language of Oman, but English is widely understood.[4] Most signs are written in both Arabic and English. Baluchi, Urdu, Swahili, Farsi, and French are also spoken in Oman, as are numerous dialects of various South Asian and Semitic languages.[5] Some easy words in Arabic are *marhaba* (welcome), *shukran* (thanks), *lau sama'at* (please), *na'am* (yes), and *la* (no). The author of the first Arabic dictionary, *Kitab al Ayn,* was from Oman. His name was Abu Abd a'Rahman Khalil ibn Ahmad al Farahidi, a linguist from the eighth century.

The importance of a tribal identity in Omani and Arab society is reflected in how the natives write their names.[3] For example, the long version of the name of the current sultan is Qaboos bin Said bin Taimur al Said. According to the Arab naming system, Qaboos is his first name (*ism*), Said was his father's first name (*nasab*), Taimur was his paternal grandfather's first name (*nasab*), and al Said is his tribe (*nisba*). *Bin* (or *ibn*) means "son of." Women use *bint* ("daughter of") instead.

The *nisba* can also indicate one's occupation or hometown. Some Arabs shorten their names by removing the word *bin/ibn/bint* (Qaboos Said Taimur al Said) or by simply stating their *ism* and *nisba* (Qaboos al Said).

The women of Oman are empowered and respected by their male counterparts. HM Sultan Qaboos has often stated in his speeches that a population that ignores its female half wastes 50 percent of its potential.[4] In the first year of the sultan's reign, Al Zahra, Oman's first school for girls, was established.[6]

Not only can Omani women go to the school of their choice, but they can also vote and work for a living.[4] Women make up one third of the Omani workforce, and since 2000, they have also been allowed to drive taxis for both male and female passengers.[7] Omani women even hold important government positions. In honor of its women, Oman celebrates October 17 as Omani Women's Day.[4]

Omani men wear simple long cotton robes called *dishdashas.* These are usually white, but they can also be black, blue, brown, lilac, or another color. The sleeves are long and loose at the cuff, and the neck is simple and round with a button. Perfume is applied to a tassel called a *furakha* or *karkusha* that dangles from the right side of the neck. Under the *dishdasha,* a simple piece of cloth called the *wizar* is wrapped around the body, covering from the waist to the ankles.

On formal occasions, a black or beige cloak called a *bisht* with intricate silver or gold embroidery along the edges may be worn over the *dishdasha.* An embroidered cap called a *kummah* or a cloth turban called a *muzzah* can be used to cover the head. A walking stick (*assa*) is often carried as an accessory, and sandals (*na'al*) are preferred over shoes and socks because they keep the feet cool.[2]

Khanjars (daggers) are reserved for special occasions. Originally worn for protection, these handcrafted silver daggers now signify male elegance. They can be worn on a *sapta,* which is a belt made of leather and silver, or held in place by a strip of cloth called a *shal* that is made of the same cloth as the *muzzah.* The khanjar can be worn without a headdress or with a *muzzah,* but never with a *kummah.* Khanjars come in various designs, but the Al Saidi khanjar is worn only by members of the Omani royal family.[2]

An Omani man wearing a *dishdasha* and carrying a khanjar on his waist

Omani women wear a *dishdasha* (also called a *thawb*) with trousers (*sirwaal*) and a headdress (*lihaf*). The length of the *dishdasha* varies from knee-length in the Batinah and Dakhiliyah to below-knee-length in the Sharqiyah to full-length in the Dhahirah. In Dhofar, long loose velvet dresses called *abu dhayl* (father of a tail) with short tails (*al dhayl*) substitute the *dishdasha*.[8]

Shawls are worn as headdresses in various styles across the country, and each style has a different name, like the *shayla* in the Batinah, the *shabaka* in Dhofar, and the *shader al tarh* in the Sharqiyah. Bedouin women often cover their faces with a mask called a *burqa,* which protects them from the sun and the sand in the desert.[2]

Traditional Omani jewelry—such as necklaces, bracelets, anklets, rings, earrings, headdresses, and amulet holders—is made of silver, but gold has gained popularity in recent years. Omani ornaments are usually chunky and ornate and are often engraved with Quranic calligraphy.[3] Nizwa, the old capital of Oman, is still famous for its silversmiths.

The most popular folk tradition of Oman is the Razha, a sword dance that is accompanied by poetry and drums. Originally a dance of war, it is now performed to welcome the sultan. Some of Oman's

Gold jewelry

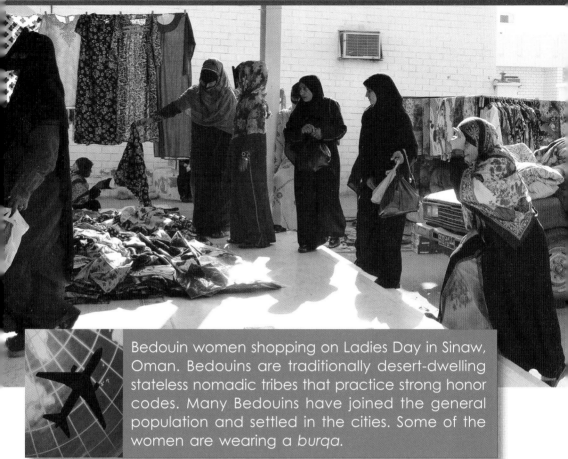

Bedouin women shopping on Ladies Day in Sinaw, Oman. Bedouins are traditionally desert-dwelling stateless nomadic tribes that practice strong honor codes. Many Bedouins have joined the general population and settled in the cities. Some of the women are wearing a *burqa*.

other folk traditions are the Bar'aa (a synchronized dagger dance from Dhofar) and women's group songs and dances like the Raqs al Nisaa from Dhofar and the Al Wailah from the Dhahirah. Songs from the Sharqiyah sing about the sea, while the old desert songs praise the camel. In the Dakhiliyah, the Taymina is sung when a child has committed the Quran to memory.[9]

Since 1988, the country's Omanization program has been encouraging employers to train and hire Omani citizens.[10] Young Omanis only have to wait until the age of 13 to get a job. Weekends in Oman fall on Thursdays and Fridays (Friday is the Muslim holy day), but some employers offer weekends on Fridays and Saturdays. Many offices still offer an afternoon break from 1:00 P.M. to 4:00 P.M., and, during the holy month of Ramadhan, students and employees enjoy reduced hours.

Allahu akbar, (x4)
Ash hadu an la ilaha illal lah, (x2)
Ash hadu anna Muhammadan rasulullah, (x2)
Hayya alas salaah, (x2)
Hayya alal falaah, (x2)
Allahu akbar, (x2)
La ilaha illal lah. (x1)
(Allah is greater than any description,
I testify that there is no deity except for Allah,
I testify that Muhammad is a Messenger of Allah,
The time for prayer has come,
The time for worship has come,
Allah is greater than any description,
There is no deity except for Allah.)

The Sultan Qaboos Grand Mosque prayer hall
also holds the Carpet of Wonder. The chandelier
above the prayer hall is 46 feet (14 meters) tall.
The design of the mosque was finalized after a
competition in 1993.

Chapter 8

The Role of Islam

Five times a day, the Islamic call to prayer—the *adhan*—rings out from the over 10,000 mosques scattered across Oman. The words are the same as the ones used in mosques all over the world.

Some of the most beautiful of these mosques can be found in Oman. The oldest is the Al Midhmar mosque in Sumail. Many of these mosques are very old; some are from when Oman embraced Islam in the seventh century.[1]

The largest mosque in Oman is the Sultan Qaboos Grand Mosque. Its five minarets represent the five pillars of Islam and the five daily prayers.[1] Until recently, the mosque held the record for having the largest Persian carpet in the world. (It has since been surpassed by another carpet in the UAE.) This 5,194-square-yard (4,342-square-meter) carpet, the Carpet of Wonder, covers the floor of the main prayer hall. It took weavers four years to make the 1.7 billion knots. The mosque also contains a library, an institute for Islamic studies, and a large lecture hall.[1]

Oman was the first country to accept Islam in 630 CE. Today Islam forms an integral part of the day-to-day lives of its people. Seventy-five percent of Omanis belong to the Ibadhi Muslim sect, with Sunni Muslims forming the next largest religious group. Small numbers of Shia Muslims, Hindus, Christians, and other communities form the rest of the population.[2] The sultan's commitment to his people extends to the Basic Law that protects human rights and guarantees freedom of religion as long as it does not cause public disorder. In addition to

At a Quranic school in Kumzar, Oman, a boy studies the Arabic alphabet. Arabic, like Hebrew, is a Semitic language, and has lent many words to English, such as alcohol (*al quhl*), algebra (*al jabr*), and cotton (*qutun*).

the numerous *masjids* (mosques) available to the Muslims, various temples and churches have also been built in Oman.[3]

Omani culture is deeply embedded in its Islamic roots. Education, for instance, contains both secular and religious dimensions. Verses from the Quran are often quoted wherever appropriate. Teachers are expected to draw inspiration from both traditional and modern sources, combining the old and the new, in order to deliver both character training and knowledge to their students.[4]

Muslims consider studying to be a religious duty, and the people of Oman are no exception. Students (boys and girls) can choose to study at a local school, international school, religious school, or even a special needs school. Scholarships are available for those in need and for those who want to study abroad. Oman's only public university, the Sultan Qaboos University, was opened in 1986. It offers students a chance to specialize in any field of their choice. Students can also enroll at any of Oman's private universities and technical institutes.[3]

The major Islamic festivals in Oman are Eid al Fitr (Festival of the Breaking of the Fast) and Eid al Adha (Festival of Sacrifice). These are celebrated by Muslims all over the world (the Arabic word *eid* means "festivity"). Muslims greet each other on these days by saying, "Eid Mubarak" (Blessed Festivity). Oman also observes Lailat al Mi'raj (Night of the Prophet's Ascent), the Islamic New Year, the birthday of the Prophet, and Ramadhan, which is the Islamic holy month of fasting.

Eid al Fitr marks the end of Ramadhan and is celebrated on the first three days of the month of Shawwal. Eid al Adha celebrations also go on for three days, starting on the tenth day of Dhu al Hijja at the end of the Hajj, the Islamic pilgrimage to Mecca, Saudi Arabia. For this festival, Muslims sacrifice a goat, camel, sheep, or cow in remembrance of Abraham's obedience to Allah (God).[5] According to

Muslim men, both Omani and otherwise, bend in prayer outside a mosque in Muscat for Eid al Fitr. Muslims around the world celebrate Eid al Fitr to mark the end of the Islamic holy month of Ramadhan.

the Quran, Allah tested Abraham by asking him to sacrifice his son, Ishmael (Ismail), to Him. Abraham passed the test by intention alone, and Allah rescued Ishmael by sending a ram in his place, which Abraham offered as thanks. Muslims today divide their sacrificial meat into thirds: one for their family; one for their relatives, friends, or neighbors; and one for the poor.

The Eid festivals are occasions of great joy all over the Muslim world. Special morning prayers are held on the first day. People meticulously clean their homes, cook special food, wear crisp new clothing, and spend time with their loved ones. Children look forward to these festivals because of the gifts and small amounts of money that the adults are expected to give them.

In Oman, festivals like Eid call for special dishes like *shuwa*—whole goat or cow marinated with spices and wrapped with dry banana or palm leaves. On the first day of Eid, the meat begins to bake in a

In accordance with the 40th Renaissance Day of Oman, Ma'edathul Nu'aman Catering services prepared chicken kabsa (biryani) in an 8.17-ton vessel, which could be consumed by about 70,000 people. This vessel has been verified by Guinness World Records as the "biggest vessel ever."

special oven in a pit in the ground. It is unearthed and eaten on the third day. On the first day of Eid, people usually eat *haris* (wheat mixed with meat), and on the second day, they feast on *mishkak* (skewered meat cooked over charcoal).[4] Other popular festival foods are *ruz al mudhroub* (rice served with fried fish), *maqdeed* (special dried meat), *muqalab* (tripe and pluck, which are the innards of an animal, cooked with spices), and *arsia* (lamb meat cooked with rice).[6]

Ramadhan is the ninth month of the Islamic calendar, and Muslims observe it with daily fasts that last from dawn to dusk. Not only do they abstain from any food or drink, but they also seek to purify themselves with additional prayers and good deeds. The first verses of the Quran were also revealed during Ramadhan. During this month in Oman, it is against the law to eat or drink anything in public—so most restaurants close in the daytime. Schools and offices also function on reduced hours.[5]

In Salalah, tourists can visit what some say are the tombs of the Prophet Job (Ayoub) and Samri, a famous magician from the time of Moses (Moosa).[7] Many people in Oman believe in magic; in Dhofar the women wear dresses with tails that wipe away their footprints so that spells may not be cast on them. The town of Bahla near Nizwa has the reputation of being the sorcery capital of Oman.[8]

Tomb of the Prophet Job (Ayoub) in Salalah, Dhofar. Both the Bible and the Quran speak of Job as a prosperous man who demonstrated great patience when his wealth, family, and health were taken away from him.

Jewelry, incense, handicrafts, and clothes—these are just some of the things tourists can begin to spend their *rials* on at the *souq* in Muttrah. Would you buy a *bisht* (cloak) like this one?

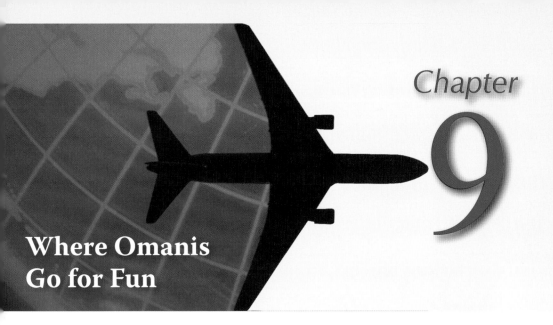

Where Omanis
Go for Fun

The essence of Oman lingers among the old-style gold, silver, pottery, clothing, and incense shops of its *souqs* (bazaars).[1] Tourists can spend hours within the alleyways of these markets discovering the sights, sounds, and smells of the old country. They can fill their shopping bags here with mementos that let them take a piece of Oman back with them. The most famous *souqs* are in Muttrah, Nizwa, and Salalah, and others sell meat, camels, fish, and goats exclusively.

Oman's rich tradition in handicrafts is always on display at its *souqs*. Weapons such as shields, swords, and khanjars; jewelry; and coffee pots made of silver and copper are strewn there in abundance, as are a variety of woven items made from date-palm leaves, cotton, wool, silk, and the hair of camels, goats, and sheep.[2] This is where visitors can choose to take home the traditional red-and-black rugs and blankets from Ibri and the clay incense burners from Dhofar.

The Omanis have always been expert shipbuilders. Their handmade ships, which are called dhows, can last for up to 100 years.[3] Muscat, Muttrah, Sur, and Sohar are Oman's main shipbuilding centers.[1] Other local skills include bone carving, leatherwork, yarn spinning, and making *jirz* axes.[4] Woodcarving is practiced as an art form, as is evident from the beautiful doors that have graced many Omani homes through the years.

Old folktales claim Sohar to be the hometown of Sinbad the Sailor and the place from where he set out on the adventures compiled in *One Thousand and One Nights* (also known as *Arabian Nights*).[5] British

Omani dhows are of many types, like the *ghanjah*, the *boum*, the *badan*, and the *sambuq*. The largest is the *baghlah*. The *sambuq* is the most common kind of dhow with its low, curved, scimitar-shaped stem piece.

explorer Tim Severin built a dhow called Sohar and re-created the voyage of Sinbad by sailing to China in 1980. The dhow now sits at a traffic circle at the entrance to the Al Bustan Palace InterContinental Hotel.

A real-life Omani sailor was Ahmed bin Majid, who grew famous in the West for helping Portuguese explorer Vasco da Gama sail from Africa to India using an Arab map unknown in Europe at the time. Ahmed bin Majid was born into a seafaring family in 1421 in Julphar (now in the UAE). The Arabs honor his courage, strength, and skills as a navigator and cartographer by calling him the first Arab seaman and *Shehan al Dein* (Lion of the Sea).[6]

Ahmed bin Majid wrote almost forty works of poetry and prose in addition to several books on the movements of ships and oceanography. Two of his handwritten books are on display at the National Library in Paris. He wrote his most famous book, *Kitab al Fawa'id fi Usul 'Ilm al Bahr wa 'l Qawa'id* (Book of Useful Information on the Principles and Rules of Navigation), in 1490. His work helped Gulf traders sail to places such as India and East Africa.[6]

In 2009, Mohsin al Busaidi became the first Omani and Arab to sail nonstop around the world.[4] Records were also set in 2009 by Nabil al Busaidi, who became the first Arab to reach the North Magnetic Pole, and in 2010 by Khalid al Siyabi, the first Omani to climb Mount Everest.[4] Bank executive and mother of three, Muna al Shanfari became the first Omani woman to climb Mount Kilimanjaro in 2010. In 2002, Najiyyah bint Khalfan bin Mubarak al Mawali became the first Omani and Gulf female pilot. She is also a professional equestrian who has competed alongside men in horse races spanning over 60 miles (100 kilometers) in the desert.[7]

The Omanis like to keep the traditional games of Al Sayyad, Al Yous, Al Lakad, and Al Quraie alive in the form of interregional competitions.[8] They also participate in mainstream world sporting events, including the Olympics, the Asian Youth Games, the University Games, and the Asian Martial Arts Games.[4]

Soccer (called football there) has a huge fan following in Oman. The Omani soccer team won the 19th Gulf Cup in 2009. Other sports that are popular with the Omanis are horse racing, car racing, sailing, cricket, golf, volleyball, tennis, and weight lifting. In 2008, Muscat held the distinction of being the only Middle Eastern capital the Olympic Torch had passed through that year. Of the 80 torchbearers in Muscat, 57 were Omani.[4]

Oman also hosts a number of sporting events every year. The Fahal Island Swim is held in May, and bullfights are held in the winter months. Horse riders can compete at the Annual Royal Meeting every winter and at the Royal Equestrian Show every five years. Camel races are an important Omani tradition and are popular the whole year round. These races can span many days, and winners can take home over half a million dollars![5]

Every April, Oman's biggest motorsport event, the Rally Oman, attracts contenders from all over the world to race in timed stages in Muscat and in Wattayah. The Wahibas Challenge also invites participants every October to test their endurance by crossing about 31 dune ridges over 37 miles (60 kilometers) of the Sharqiyah Desert in a four-wheeler.[5]

Since 1998, Oman's capital city has been hosting the Muscat Festival, a 22-day-long carnival that is held every year in January and February at a number of locations across the city. Visitors from Oman

At the Sultan Qaboos port at the Muscat Corniche drive, visitors like to spend their time shopping at the nearby Muttrah *souq* in the day and enjoying the sea breeze while on a stroll with their families and friends in the evening.

and overseas turn out in large numbers for the chance to experience Oman's heritage at this festival, where one can spend hours cruising food and shopping stalls from all over the world and also enjoy games, camel races, dances, concerts, and art workshops.[7]

Salalah hosts a similar festival every year from July 15 to the end of August to mark the arrival of the annual *khareef* (monsoon). Visitors can escape to a Dhofari summer—cool, misty, and green—and immerse themselves in Omani handicrafts, dance, and music at the award-winning Salalah Tourist Festival.[7]

In 2001, Oman became the first Persian Gulf country to host its own film festival. The Muscat Film Festival is held every two years and is attended by film personalities from all over the world. Multiple locations across Muscat screen short and feature-length films from Arab and international cinema. In 2010, the festival was attended by a number of Indian celebrities, including famous Bollywood actor Amitabh Bachchan and Oscar-winning sound editor Resul Pookutty.

Omani children enjoy the day at an amusement park on the second day of Eid al Fitr in Muscat as Muslim families continue to celebrate the end of Ramadhan, the holy month of fasting.

Visitors also enjoy taking a tour of some of Oman's most famous landmarks, such as the Al Alam Royal Palace, the gold-plated door of the Oman International Bank, and the award-winning Al Bustan Palace InterContinental Hotel, which is set upon 200 acres (81 hectares) of private beach and gardens. The options don't end there; visitors can continue exploring Oman through its various museums, parks, and modern shopping centers.

All that remains is that first step of your journey toward this corner of Arabia. Where will you begin? What part of Oman beckons you? For some, it is the ancient passions of its people. For others, it is the elusive mists of Dhofar. Many have forgotten themselves in the night-time stillness of the desert that never seems to end. The coffee is strong here, and the dates are sweet. Few have ever been able to undo the spell that this country casts on them. What about Oman will charm you?

Halwa symbolizes the generosity of the people of Oman who have been welcoming guests into their homes for generations. The word *halwa* is Arabic for "sweet," and it is not unusual to hear Arabic speakers exclaim *"Halwa!"* to express happiness. The best *halwa* is prepared by professional *halwa* makers, who mix the ingredients in secret proportions and stir them for at least a couple of hours in a large container called a *mirjnl* over a fire made of special wood called *snmr*. It is served in a bowl called a *dist*. This *halwa* can be preserved as is for over four months, even without refrigeration.

Ingredients

½ teaspoon saffron
1 teaspoon cardamom powder
4 tablespoons rosewater
1¾ cups cornstarch
10 cups water
3¾ cups white sugar

¾ cup brown sugar
½ cup cashew nuts
½ cup pistachios
¼ cup ghee (clarified butter, available at health food stores)
extra cashews and pistachios for garnish

Instructions

1. In a small bowl, soak the saffron and cardamom powder in the rosewater.
2. In another bowl, dissolve the cornstarch in half the water.
3. In a pot, mix the two types of sugar in the remaining water. Bring the mixture to a boil.
4. Add the cornstarch mixture to the pot.
5. Stir continuously over low heat for 1 to 1½ hours.
6. Add the soaked saffron and cardamom powder to the pot. Also add the cashew nuts, pistachios, and ghee. Stir the mixture.
7. Pour the contents of the pot into a casserole dish that is 1 to 2 inches deep. Let the *halwa* cool and set. Garnish with more nuts.

Omani Watchtower

The Omani people have long watched over their country from behind strategically located watchtowers. Some watchtowers were part of a fort or a castle, while others stood on their own, at the entrance to a city, or atop a mountain. The Sumail Gap in the Hajar Mountains connects the coast with the interior and is littered with watchtowers from which soldiers could monitor the movements of travelers and invaders. A casual drive through the country today will still yield a number of old watchtowers, some that have long been abandoned, others that are still in use. Some famous forts are even featured on Omani currency and postage stamps. Many modern buildings in Oman are built to look like forts and watchtowers, with battlements as the popular feature.

Supplies

Pencil with eraser
Empty toilet paper roll
White paper
Clear tape
Scissors
Matte knife
An adult
Toothpick
Markers (red, green, and black)
Ruler

Instructions

1. Using a pencil, lightly mark doors, windows, and typical Omani fort battlements on the toilet paper roll.
2. Using scissors, a matte knife, and the help of **an adult**, neatly cut out the design on the toilet paper roll.
3. Decorate and outline the cutout edges with a black marker. Erase any remaining pencil marks. Set it aside.
4. Cut out a small rectangular piece of white paper for the flag. Adjust the size according to the size of the roll.
5. Draw the Omani flag on the paper using a pencil and a ruler. Fill in the colors with red and green markers.
6. Attach one end of a toothpick to the back of the flag with a small piece of tape. Tape the flag to the watchtower.

BCE

1,000,000–10,000 Early Stone Age in Oman.

10,000–3000 Late Stone Age. Wattayah near Muscat is the site of the oldest human settlements, which date back to 10,000 BCE.

3000–2000 Early Bronze Age. The cultures of Hafit (2,900–2,500) and Umm a'Nar (2,700–2,000) occupy northern Oman.

3000–100 CE Wubar flourishes in southern Oman as a frankincense trade port.

2500–2000 The Magan/Makkan period. Sumerian cuneiform texts mention the land of Magan/Makkan (possibly Oman) as a source of copper and diorite for Mesopotamia.

2000–1000 Late Bronze Age. The transitional Wadi Suq culture (2,000–1,000) survives the Umm a'Nar. The cultures of al Wasit (1,500–1,200) and Nizwa (1,200–1,000) occupy northern Oman.

c. 1000 The Persians introduce *aflaaj* to Oman.

1000–100 Early Iron Age. The Lizq culture (1,200–200) inhabits central Oman.

100–630 CE Late Iron Age. The Samad culture (100–893CE) occupies central Oman.

c. 600 The Mazoon period. The Persians begin to exert control over Oman until the arrival of Islam in the 7th century CE.

CE

200 Triliths in Semitic non-Arabic tribal territory in southern Oman are inscribed with an undecipherable south-Arabic script.

630 Oman accepts Islam during the lifetime of the Prophet Muhammad.

661–750 Oman becomes a part of the Umayyad caliphate, the largest Arab-Muslim state in history. Their capital is Damascus, the modern-day capital of Syria.

750–967 The Abbasid caliphate of Baghdad (now in Iraq) rules over Oman.

751 Ibadhi Muslims establish an imamate in Oman.

931–1154 Oman falls under the control of the Arab Qarmatians (931–934), the Persian Buyids (967–1053), and the Turco-Persian Seljuqs of Kirman (1053–1154).

1154–1624 The indigenous Nabhan dynasty intermittently rules over Oman.

1507–1650 Portugal conquers Muscat (1507) and the Strait of Hormuz (1515). It controls Oman until the natives expel the Portuguese in 1650.

1624–1744 The Yarubi period. The country is renamed Muscat and Oman.

1744–1749 Invasions by the Ottoman Turks and the Persians (1737) are countered by Ahmed bin Said, who becomes imam and founds the Busaidi dynasty. The Omani Empire expands to East Africa and the Indian subcontinent.

1793 The capital of the Omani Empire shifts from Rustaq to Muscat.

1832 Zanzibar becomes the second capital of the Omani Empire.

1856 The Omani Empire splits into its East African provinces and Muscat and Oman.

1890 Muscat and Oman becomes a British Protectorate.

1913–1959 The imam and the sultan resume clashes over control of the interior. Sultan Said bin Taimur prevails with the help of the British and expels the last imam.

1964 Oil is discovered in Oman. Extraction begins in 1967.

1965 Antigovernment communist rebels form the Dhofar Liberation Front.

1970 HM Sultan Qaboos ascends to the throne on July 23.

1971 Oman becomes a member of the United Nations and the Arab League.

1975 HM Sultan Qaboos defeats the Dhofar Liberation Front.

1981 The State Consultative Council (Majlis al Istishari lil Dawla) is created. Oman becomes a founding member of the Gulf Cooperation Council (GCC).

1984 Space shuttle *Challenger* turns up images of Wubar.

1986 Oman's first university, the Sultan Qaboos University, opens.

1991 The Consultative Council (Majlis a'Shura) replaces the State Consultative Council (Majlis al Istishari lil Dawla).

1996 HM Sultan Qaboos establishes the Basic Law of the State.

1997 The State Council (Majlis a'Dawla) is established, and together with the Consultative Council (Majlis a'Shura), comprises the Council of Oman (Majlis Oman).

2002 Voting rights are extended to all Omani citizens over the age of 21.

2003 First elections are held for the Consultative Council (Majlis a'Shura).

2005 Thirty-one Omani Islamists are tried for attempting to overthrow the government. They are pardoned.

2006 Oman and the United States sign a free trade deal, effective January 2009.

2007 Cyclone Gonu kills over 50 people and disrupts oil production in Oman.

2008 The Olympic torch arrives in Oman.

2009 The last imam dies in exile.

2010 Oman celebrates 40 years of renaissance under HM Sultan Qaboos.

2011 Protesters in Sohar and Muscat demand economic and political reforms. They do not challenge the rule of HM Sultan Qaboos. The sultan responds by promising more jobs, reshuffling his cabinet, and granting more legislative powers to the Consultative Council (Majlis a'Shura), among other reforms.

Introduction
1. Matthew McCann Fenton, *The Middle East* (New York: TIME Books, 2006), pp. 8, 18–19, 60–61, 64.
2. Anne Bouji, *This Is Oman* (Muscat, Sultanate of Oman: Al Roya Publishing, 2003), pp. 10–11.

Chapter 1. Oman Overview
1. Anne Bouji, *This Is Oman* (Muscat, Sultanate of Oman: Al Roya Publishing, 2003), pp. 16, 93–94.
2. Pauline Shelton. *The Heritage of Oman* (Berkshire, UK: Garnet Publishing Limited, 1995), pp. 18–19, 28–29, 42.
3. Pauline Searle, *Dawn Over Oman* (London: George Allen and Unwin Ltd., 1979), p. 4.
4. Mohammed bin Suleiman Al Hadrahmi, *Oman: Years of Progress and Development* (Muscat, Sultanate of Oman: Ministry of Information, 2005), pp. 14, 19.
5. Yousuf M. Budd, *Oman 2009–2010* (Muscat, Sultanate of Oman: Ministry of Information, 2009), pp. 12, 19, 136, 152–153, 253, 263.

Chapter 2. Since the Time of Frankincense
1. Anne Bouji, *This Is Oman* (Muscat, Sultanate of Oman: Al Roya Publishing, 2003), pp. 12, 14, 16, 93–94, 117.
2. Pauline Shelton, *The Heritage of Oman* (Berkshire, UK: Garnet Publishing Limited, 1995), pp. 15, 18–37, 42, 54–61, 78, 92, 103, 128.
3. Mohammed bin Suleiman Al Hadrahmi, *Oman: Years of Progress and Development* (Muscat, Sultanate of Oman: Ministry of Information, 2005), pp. 10, 12, 88, 101–105, 130, 156, 168–169, 321.
4. Yousuf M. Budd, *Oman 2009–2010* (Muscat, Sultanate of Oman: Ministry of Information, 2009), pp. 13, 19, 38, 40–41.
5. Lucie Cruickshank, *Oman Mini Explorer* (Dubai, United Arab Emirates: Explorer Publishing and Distribution, 2008), pp. 22, 98.
6. Ahmed Hamoud Al Maamiry, *Whither Oman* (New Delhi: Lancers Publishers, 1981), pp. 2–4, 9–13.

Chapter 3. An Empire by the Sea
1. Anne Bouji, *This Is Oman* (Muscat, Sultanate of Oman: Al Roya Publishing, 2003), pp. 34–35, 81–83, 97, 104.
2. Dr. Mohammed Saber Arab, *Glimpses of the History of Oman* (Muscat, Sultanate of Oman: Ministry of Information, 2000), pp. 7, 10, 20, 48–49.
3. Pauline Shelton, *The Heritage of Oman* (Berkshire, UK: Garnet Publishing Limited, 1995), pp. 25–26, 59, 96, 118.
4. Ahmed Hamoud Al Maamiry, *Whither Oman* (New Delhi: Lancers Publishers, 1981), pp. 2–4, 9–13.
5. Lucie Cruickshank, *Oman Mini Explorer* (Dubai, United Arab Emirates: Explorer Publishing and Distribution, 2008), pp. 182, 184.

6. Yousuf M. Budd, *Oman 2009–2010* (Muscat, Sultanate of Oman: Ministry of Information, 2009), pp. 38, 40–41.
7. Pauline Searle, *Dawn Over Oman* (London: George Allen and Unwin Ltd., 1979), pp. 15, 19, 22–25.

Chapter 4. Extreme Geography
1. Mohammed bin Suleiman Al Hadrahmi, *Oman: Years of Progress and Development* (Muscat, Sultanate of Oman: Ministry of Information, 2005), pp. 14–24, 199, 392–393.
2. Lucie Cruickshank, *Oman Mini Explorer* (Dubai, United Arab Emirates: Explorer Publishing and Distribution, 2008), pp. 22, 98, 102–109.
3. Anne Bouji, *This Is Oman* (Muscat, Sultanate of Oman: Al Roya Publishing, 2003), pp. 12, 30, 43–49, 71, 73, 87.
4. Pauline Shelton, *The Heritage of Oman* (Berkshire, UK: Garnet Publishing Limited, 1995), pp. 15, 25–26, 59, 92, 96, 103, 118.
5. Sultanate of Oman Ministry of Information: Tourism, "Falaj and Springs," http://www.omanet.om/english/tourism/eco/falaj.asp?cat=tourandsubcat=ecoo1
6. Salim T.S. Al Hassani, *1001 Inventions: Muslim Heritage in Our World* (Manchester: Foundation for Science, Technology and Civilisation, 2007), p. 190.

Chapter 5. The Land and Its Resources
1. Anne Bouji, *This Is Oman* (Muscat, Sultanate of Oman: Al Roya Publishing, 2003), pp. 19, 32, 43–49, 71, 87, 88, 108.
2. Pauline Shelton, *The Heritage of Oman* (Berkshire, UK: Garnet Publishing Limited, 1995), pp. 18–37, 42, 54–61, 78, 128.
3. Sultanate of Oman Ministry of Information: Economy, Water Resources, http://www.omanet.om/english/commerce/econ11.asp?cat=comm
4. Mohammed bin Suleiman Al Hadrahmi, *Oman: Years of Progress and Development* (Muscat, Sultanate of Oman: Ministry of Information, 2005), pp. 10, 12, 14–24, 199, 392–393.
5. Dr. Mohammed Saber Arab, *Glimpses of the History of Oman* (Muscat, Sultanate of Oman: Ministry of Information, 2000), pp. 7, 10, 20, 48–49.
6. Sultanate of Oman Ministry of Information: Economy, Agriculture, Fisheries, and Livestock, http://www.omanet.om/cnglish/commerce/econ8.asp?cat=comm
7. Yousuf M. Budd, *Oman 2009–2010* (Muscat, Sultanate of Oman: Ministry of Information, 2009), pp. 190, 200, 208–213.
8. Pauline Searle, *Dawn Over Oman* (London: George Allen and Unwin Ltd., 1979), pp. 40, 80.
9. CIA: *The World Factbook,* "Oman," https://www.cia.gov/library/publications/the-world-factbook/geos/mu.html

10. Sultanate of Oman Ministry of Information: Culture, Horse Breeding, http://www.omanet.om/english/culture/hors2.asp?cat=cultandsubcat=cult2

Chapter 6. A Royal Legacy

1. Mohammed bin Suleiman Al Hadrahmi, *Oman: Years of Progress and Development* (Muscat, Sultanate of Oman: Ministry of Information, 2005), pp. 26–39, 42, 56–65, 335.
2. Lucie Cruickshank, *Oman Mini Explorer* (Dubai, United Arab Emirates: Explorer Publishing and Distribution, 2008), pp. 28–30.
3. Shelton, Pauline. *The Heritage of Oman* (Berkshire, UK: Garnet Publishing Limited, 1995), p. 142.
4. Pauline Searle, *Dawn Over Oman* (London: George Allen and Unwin Ltd., 1979), pp. 15, 19, 22–25.
5. Yousuf M. Budd, *Oman 2009–2010* (Muscat, Sultanate of Oman: Ministry of Information, 2009), pp. 44–45, 62–83, 86–93, 96–104, 118–132, 159.
6. Ahmed Hamoud Al Maamiry, *Whither Oman* (New Delhi: Lancers Publishers, 1981), pp. 47, 51–53, 74.

Chapter 7. Arab Generosity

1. Ahmed Hamoud Al Maamiry, *Whither Oman* (New Delhi: Lancers Publishers, 1981), pp. 23, 31–34, 42–44.
2. Anne Bouji, *This Is Oman* (Muscat, Sultanate of Oman: Al Roya Publishing, 2003), pp. 10, 18–20, 22–27, 40–41.
3. Pauline Searle, *Dawn Over Oman* (London: George Allen and Unwin Ltd., 1979), pp. 12, 115–120.
4. Yousuf M. Budd, *Oman 2009–2010* (Muscat, Sultanate of Oman: Ministry of Information, 2009), pp. 46–47, 86, 136–148, 157–165, 182, 262.
5. CIA: *The World Factbook,* "Oman," https://www.cia.gov/library/publications/the-world-factbook/geos/mu.html
6. Arab Women Organization, Milestones, http://english.arabwomenorg.com/Milestones.html
7. "Omani Women Take a Front Seat," *BBC News,* May 28, 2000, http://news.bbc.co.uk/2/hi/middle_east/767732.stm
8. Sultanate of Oman Ministry of Information: Culture, "National Dress—Women," http://www.omanet.om/english/culture/women_dress.asp?cat=cult
9. Sultanate of Oman Ministry of Information: Culture, "Folk Songs and Dances," http://www.omanet.om/english/culture/folk_song.asp?cat=cult
10. Sultanate of Oman Ministry of Information: Omanisation Policy, http://www.omanet.om/english/misc/omanise.asp

Chapter 8. The Role of Islam

1. Mohammed bin Suleiman Al Hadrahmi, *Oman: Years of Progress and Development* (Muscat, Sultanate of Oman: Ministry of Information, 2005), pp. 88, 101–105, 130, 156, 168–169, 321.
2. CIA: *The World Factbook,* "Oman," https://www.cia.gov/library/publications/the-world-factbook/geos/mu.html
3. Yousuf M. Budd, *Oman 2009–2010* (Muscat, Sultanate of Oman: Ministry of Information, 2009), pp. 62–83, 86–93, 96–104, 118–132, 136–148, 262.
4. Ahmed Hamoud Al Maamiry, *Whither Oman* (New Delhi: Lancers Publishers, 1981), pp. 23, 31–34, 42–44.
5. Lucie Cruickshank, *Oman Mini Explorer* (Dubai, United Arab Emirates: Explorer Publishing and Distribution, 2008), pp. 28–30.
6. Sultanate of Oman Ministry of Information: Culture, "Traditional Omani Food," http://www.omanet.om/english/culture/omani_food.asp?cat=cult
7. Pauline Shelton, *The Heritage of Oman* (Berkshire, UK: Garnet Publishing Limited, 1995), pp. 25–26, 59, 96, 118.
8. Anne Bouji, *This Is Oman* (Muscat, Sultanate of Oman: Al Roya Publishing, 2003), pp. 34–35, 81–83, 97, 104.

Chapter 9. Where Omanis Go for Fun

1. Mohammed bin Suleiman Al Hadrahmi, *Oman: Years of Progress and Development* (Muscat, Sultanate of Oman: Ministry of Information, 2005), pp. 88, 101–105, 130, 156, 168–169, 321, 335.
2. Pauline Shelton, *The Heritage of Oman* (Berkshire, UK: Garnet Publishing Limited, 1995), pp. 18–37, 42, 54–61, 78, 128.
3. Sultanate of Oman Ministry of Information: Culture, "Ship (Dhow) Building," http://www.omanet.om/english/culture/shipbuilding.asp?cat=cultandsubcat=cult2
4. Yousuf M. Budd, *Oman 2009–2010* (Muscat, Sultanate of Oman: Ministry of Information, 2009), pp. 44–47, 66–67, 157–165, 182, 190, 200, 208–213, 224–228.
5. Anne Bouji, *This Is Oman* (Muscat, Sultanate of Oman: Al Roya Publishing, 2003), pp. 12, 19, 30, 32, 71, 73, 88, 108.
6. Paul Lunde, "The Navigator: Ahmad ibn Majid," *Saudi Aramco World,* July/August 2005, http://www.saudiaramcoworld.com/issue/200504/the.navigator.ahmad.ibn.majid.htm
7. Arab Women Organization, Milestones, http://english.arabwomenorg.com/Milestones.html
8. Sultanate of Oman Ministry of Information: Social Development, "Sports and Youth," http://www.omanet.om/english/social/dev5.asp?cat=hist

Books

Ejaz, Khadija. *How'd They Do That in the Persian Empire?* Hockessin, Delaware: Mitchell Lane Publishers, 2010.

King, David C. *Cultures of the World: Oman.* Tarrytown, New York: Marshall Cavendish Children's Books, 2008.

Michael, Isaac. *A Historical Atlas of Oman.* New York: Rosen Publishing Group, 2004.

Todino-Gonguet, Grace. *Halimah and the Snake and Other Omani Folktales.* London: Stacey International Publishers, 2008.

Works Consulted

This book is based on the author's experiences while being raised in the Sultanate of Oman and on the following sources:

Al Hadrahmi, Mohammed bin Suleiman. *Oman: Years of Progress and Development.* Muscat, Sultanate of Oman: Ministry of Information, 2005.

Al Hassani, Salim T.S. *1001 Inventions: Muslim Heritage in Our World.* Manchester: Foundation for Science, Technology and Civilisation, 2007.

Al Maamiry, Ahmed Hamoud. *Whither Oman.* New Delhi: Lancers Publishers, 1981.

Arab, Dr. Mohammed Saber. *Glimpses of the History of Oman.* Muscat, Sultanate of Oman: Ministry of Information, 2000.

Arab Women Organization
http://english.arabwomenorg.com/

BBC News—Oman Country Profile
http://news.bbc.co.uk/2/hi/middle_east/country_profiles/791892.stm

Bouji, Anne. *This Is Oman.* Muscat, Sultanate of Oman: Al Roya Publishing, 2003.

Budd, Yousuf M. *Oman 2009–2010.* Muscat, Sultanate of Oman: Ministry of Information, 2009.

CIA: *The World Factbook,* "Oman," https://www.cia.gov/library/publications/the-world-factbook/geos/mu.html

Cooper, Stuart. *History.* Great Bardfield, Essex, UK: Bardfield Press, 2004.

Cruickshank, Lucie. *Oman Mini Explorer.* Dubai, United Arab Emirates: Explorer Publishing and Distribution, 2008.

Fenton, Matthew McCann. *The Middle East.* New York: TIME Books, 2006.

"Omani Women Take a Front Seat," *BBC News,* May 28, 2000, http://news.bbc.co.uk/2/hi/middle_east/767732.stm

Searle, Pauline. *Dawn Over Oman.* London: George Allen and Unwin Ltd., 1979.

Shelton, Pauline. *The Heritage of Oman.* Berkshire, UK: Garnet Publishing Limited, 1995.

Sultanate of Oman Ministry of Information
http://www.omanet.om

On the Internet

Destination Oman
http://www.destinationoman.com

My Oman Info
http://oman.mydestinationinfo.com

Sultanate of Oman Ministry of Culture and Heritage
http://www.mhc.gov.om/english

Sultanate of Oman Ministry of Foreign Affairs
http://www.mofa.gov.om

Sultanate of Oman Ministry of Information
http://www.omanet.om

Sultanate of Oman Ministry of Tourism
http://www.omantourism.gov.om

battalion (beh-TAAL-yen)—A military unit composed of a headquarters and two or more companies, batteries, or similar units.

bicameral (by-KAM-uh-rul)—Based on two legislative or judicial bodies.

cartographer (kar-TAH-grah-fer)—A person who makes maps.

consul (KAHN-sul)—A government official who lives in a foreign country and represents the commercial interests of his or her own country.

cuneiform (kyoo-NEE-ih-form)—Composed of or written in wedge-shaped characters.

desalination (dee-sal-ih-NAY-shun)—The process of removing salt.

diversification (dih-ver-seh-fih-KAY-shun)—Balancing an economy by dividing it among different industries.

dynasty (DY-nus-tee)—A line of rulers from the same family.

ecosystem (EH-koh-sis-tem)—A community of organisms and their environment working together as a natural unit.

envoy (ON-voy)—A person who represents one government in its dealings with another.

exclave (EX-klayv)—A portion of a country separated from the main part.

fjord (FYORD)—A valley formed by melting glaciers that cut into rock.

gulf (GULF)—A part of an ocean or sea that extends into the land.

Ibadhi (ih-BAH-dee)—A form of Islam distinct from the Sunni and Shia forms.

imamate (ee-MAA-mut)—A region ruled by an imam.

incense (IN-sents)—Material used to produce a fragrant odor when burned.

indigenous (in-DIH-juh-nus)—Originally from (a particular region).

infantry (IN-fen-tree)—Soldiers trained, armed, and equipped to fight on foot.

jinn (JIN)—Any of a class of hidden beings that occupy the Earth, according to Islam.

jirz (JIRZ)—A small long-handled ax from Musandam.

linguist (LIN-gwist)—A person who specializes in languages.

mausoleum (mah-zuh-LEE-um)—A large building for housing tombs.

minaret (mih-nuh-RET)—A tall, slender tower on a mosque.

monsoon (mon-SOON)—Heavy rain brought by seasonal winds from the Indian Ocean.

necropolis (neh-KRAH-puh-lis)—A large elaborate cemetery of an ancient city.

nomad (NOH-mad)—A person who has no fixed home but moves from place to place, usually seasonally and within a certain area.

oceanography (oh-shuh-NAH-gruh-fee)—The study of the oceans, including their extent, depth, physics, chemistry, biology, and resources.

peninsula (peh-NIN-suh-lah)—A piece of land that is nearly surrounded by water.

quinquireme (KWIN-kwee-rem)—A type of Roman warship that had five banks of oars on each side.

Quran (kur-ON)—The holy book of Islam.

renaissance (REH-nuh-zahntz)—A period of artistic and intellectual awakening.

secular (SEH-kyoo-ler)—Separate from religious doctrine.

Semitic (seh-MIH-tik)—Relating to the people (Semites) who spoke one of the Afro-Asiatic languages, such as Hebrew, Aramaic, Arabic, or Amharic.

sultanate (SUL-tuh-nut)—A state governed by a sultan.

UNESCO (yoo-NES-koh)—United Nations Educational, Scientific, and Cultural Organization; an agency of the United Nations that promotes international dialogue through education, the sciences, culture, communication, and information.

water table—The surface of the groundwater in a given area.

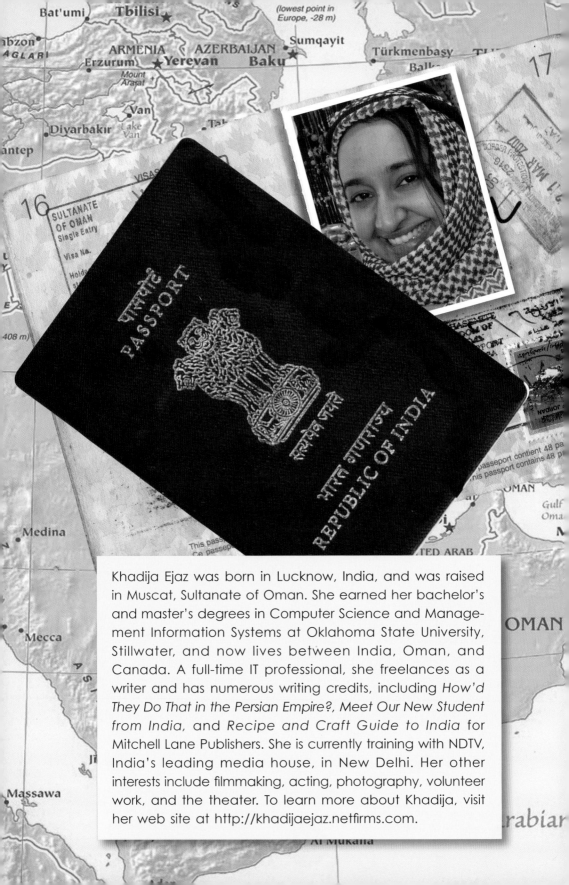

Khadija Ejaz was born in Lucknow, India, and was raised in Muscat, Sultanate of Oman. She earned her bachelor's and master's degrees in Computer Science and Management Information Systems at Oklahoma State University, Stillwater, and now lives between India, Oman, and Canada. A full-time IT professional, she freelances as a writer and has numerous writing credits, including *How'd They Do That in the Persian Empire?*, *Meet Our New Student from India*, and *Recipe and Craft Guide to India* for Mitchell Lane Publishers. She is currently training with NDTV, India's leading media house, in New Delhi. Her other interests include filmmaking, acting, photography, volunteer work, and the theater. To learn more about Khadija, visit her web site at http://khadijaejaz.netfirms.com.